# Dear Santa

# Dear Santa

## Letters and Drawings
## to Father Christmas

Compiled by Ron Abercrombie

MAINSTREAM
PUBLISHING

EDINBURGH AND LONDON

First published in Great Britain in 1999 by
MAINSTREAM PUBLISHING COMPANY (EDINBURGH) LTD
7 Albany Street
Edinburgh EH1 3UG

ISBN  1 84018 232 6

A catalogue record for this book is available from the British Library

Typeset in Plantin and Comic Sans
Printed in Hong Kong by H&Y Printing Ltd

# Foreword

This compilation was inspired by my daughters' letters and drawings to Santa Claus – and the presents he left us all! Their efforts feature here among the dozens from children of various ages, religions and ethnic backgrounds all in celebration of the spirit of Father Christmas. It's appropriate, therefore, that a donation from the sale of each book goes to the children of the world through the Save the Children fund.

To Brenda, Kirstin and Claire

# You Want What?

Dear Santa,

My little sister Jessica is only 9 months old and Mummy says she wants teeth for Christmas. So can you bring them along as well.

**Happy Christmas, Sam**

Dear Father Christmas,

I have been very good this year.
Please can I have some presents. I
would like a baby.

Love, Danielle

Dear Santa,

This year I have been helping around the house by putting up the decorations. I have also been playing football and I haven't hacked anybody.

For Christmas I would like a computer game for my Playstation. I would also like a marrow but they are out of season. There are many other things I want but I can't remember them all.

Merry Christmas and a Happy New Year.

From Luke

Dear Santa,
   I would like a swing and a
      bike and my mum would
      like to get married
      but wot I would like
      best is a cat.

Merry Christmas, Luchia

Dear Santa,
Please can you get

| | | |
|---|---|---|
| Lucy | = | a puppy |
| Me | = | inflatable chair |
| Nicola | = | 911 album |
| Ashley | = | a car |
| Jessica | = | Reebok trainers |
| Stephanie | = | a dog |
| Holly | = | make up |
| Laura | = | nothing |

Dear Santa Clause,

If I am a good girl will you fetch me a dollys house and a dolly who cries and we wes.

**Lots of love, Holly**

Dear Father Christmas,

My name is Sam and I am waiting for my tonsils, adenoids and gromits to be done any time.

Dear Santa,

My name is Kieran and at the moment I'm very poorly with chicken pox. Please could you bring me Lion King figures and make all my spots go away.

To Santa,

    I want a wiggley ball and a cat costume and a violin and a house that you can fit in 4 or 5 people.

              From Kenneth

Dear Santa,

I would like a brand new yoyo and lots of books. Please can you wrap them and a real chicken and a diamond ring. Please draw a picture of you. Thank you for listening.

**Love from Sara**

 ←— YOU

Dear Sinta Class,

I hope that you are OK. Thank you for my chocolate last Christmas. Please may I have a game for my Playstation.

**From Ronan**

P.S. My mum wants a limousine.

Dear Father Xmas,

I have been a very good girl this year and the thing I would like most in the world is David Beckham. I promise to be extra good if I can have it.

Yours, Sandra

Dear Father Christmas,

If I am good will you bring me a piglet and some pigs.

Love, Carla

Dear Father Christmas,

   Please may I have cuddly toy, toy to make, a new different yoyo and return tickets to Egypt.

**Happy Christmas, James**


Dear Santa,

   Please can I have a necklace and for my sister a big toy and for my mum a blouse and for my dad some land in Jamaica.

**Love, Rebecca**

# Are You Ready?

Dear Santa,
 How are you and your elves?
Are your raindeers looking fit for
 success?

**Merry Christmas, Nicholas**

Dear Santa,
 I hope you and your elves
are able to make toys in time
for Christmas. The bendy pencil was fun. This
Christmas can I have a duck feeder so I don't
have to feed the ducks.

**Thank you, Jacob**

# Instructions

Dear Father Christmas,

    Please do not forget the surprise my mum is making out of a loo roll. Don't forget to look through the angels book to check we have all been good. The tree is in the lounge. If you choose the right chimney you'll end up there anyway. If you choose the wrong one you'll end up in a pitch black hole in my bedroom wall.

From, Alex

Dear Father Christmas,

    I am trying to be a good girl so you will visit me at Christmas. I hope the fire will have gone out by then so you don't burn your bottom.

Lots of love, Jasmine

Dear Father Christmas,

   This is a sort of notice of warning!
1. Please be careful of the extremely
loud creak in the stairs. 2. And be
careful not to scare my cat
Jassie. By the way there is
some sherry and carrots for
you and the donkeys.

**From Stephanie**


Dear Santa Claus,

   I'm giving you some warnings
not that you want them but the first 4 stairs are
creaky and the door handle is stiff. Mum has
just put a new carpet down so if you get marks
on them she'll go balistick. Last but not least
your chery and mintspie are on the table. Now
less chit chat and lets get down to the basics.
This year I would like . . .

**All my love, Imogen**

You don't have to use your
magic key because we have a
chimney.

From Ben

Dear Father Christmas,

I have had a lovely year. Unfortunately I am very late writing this letter and my mum and dad have been asking me time and time again to write it. To my surprise mum and dad have bought me a present that I was going to ask you to bring. This year all my yo-yos have stopped spinning also the elves might have told you I am fasinated about rocks and there is a shop in Newton Abbot to make cabinets to your satisfaction and I have got 32 rocks!!! So think big.

Yours sincerely, Richard

# The Catering

Dear Santa,

I will leave a carrot for the reindeer and a mince pie for you and a stiff drink.

Love, Chantelle

Dear Santa,

Hi Santa how are you doing? And how's Rudolph? How's your wife doing? Want some rum then come to my house.

Yours sincerely, Craig

Dear Santa,

I will leave a drink of milk and some chicken and chips for you to eat. For Rudolph I will leave some milk to drink and chicken and beans to eat.

Love, Alice

# Since Last Year

Dear Father Christmas,

How are you doing, and Rudolph – getting enough carrots? Santa if you would like a present, what would you like and why? I've been really really good and if you don't believe me ask Mr Abbott (my English teacher). Have a nice year.

Sam, 11

To Farther Christmas,

My mum and dad say I am good most of the time, but sometimes I am a little sod.

Thank you, love from Dylan

Halow

Dear Santa,
Mummy and Daddy
said I have been a
good boy. Most of
the time.

Thomas, 6

Me (a little angel)

Dear Santa Clause,

I'll tell you the bad things I've done.

1. I punched my brother in the nose for no
reason.

2. I broke my mums favourite vase which she got
for her birthday.

3. I strangled my dog because he scratched me.

I'll now tell you what I want for Christmas.

Merry Christmas, Lucy

# C o a l!

Dear santa

this is
me

Dear Santa,
I've been
pretty good
ever since
you gave me a
piece of coal
last year, I don't
need another. I've
changed, honestly,
definately from last
year, I promise I'll
be as good as gold,
forever. By the way
we don't advise you
to come down the
chimney, so we'll leave a
key under the doormat.

**Gemma**

Dear Santa,

I've been quite good this year, though my brother hasn't. I've made my Christmas list. It's brilliant. I think my brother deserves a lump of coal. Not me this year! I haven't done anything wrong, much.

Jessica

Dear Santa,

My name is Sean and I'm trying to be good so can you bring me presents please. Santa is it true that you bring a lump of coal if the children are naughty? So if I'm naughty will I, Sean the best footballer, get one. So will Stan Collymore get one because he was naughty when Liverpool played Villa.

Love from Sean, 6

# Rudolph

Dear Father Christmas,
How are you and how is Rudolph? You know, your red nosed reindeer.

Matthew, 9

Dear Santa Claus,
How's Rudolph has he still got a red nose or has he had some Tunes?

Catherine, 10

Dear Santa,

How are you doing? I'm fine. Has Rudolph still got a red nose or has it turned blue? Is Merry Christmas still up and going? Santa do you shave? If not why not?

Amy, 11

Dear Santa

Are you and your reindears well and has Rodolph got picked on still. I love Rodolphs shiny red nose. How is Mrs Christmas as well. I wonder if your elfs are doing the presents. Please Farther Christmas can you bring me a real horse and please can you bring other children presents what they really want and my mum and dad.

Love always, from Adam

# Belief

Dear Santa,

Some of my friends do not believe in you. Please could you send me a letter to tell me what to do about it.

Yours faithfully, Matthew

Dear Santa,

I have been very good at school. I try not to be mad and well I think you are real but my friends Laura and Rebecca do not think you are real or is it the tooth fairy?

Love, Natalie

Dear Santa Claw's,

I am trying to figer out if you are true because last year I hid a mince pie without nowone watching me. The next morning I unrapped it and it was a bit eaten and not last year but the year before I went downstairs and no presents were there. It was strange because my mother looked like she had forgotten something.

Elizabeth, 8


Dear Father Christmas,

I wish you a Happy Christmas and a Happy New Year. I am six years old and I believe in you.

Love, Carmen

# Questions

Dear Santa,
How are you? I'm fine I've been doing lots of things this year. How long is your beard? My friend says it must be two meters long by now!

William, 10

Dear Santa,
How did you get to be Father Christmas? How can you get through the chimney? I wish Dad's leg can get well.

Love, Rahul

Good try.
He would not have worn Y fronts!

Dear Santa Claus,

I know it's a busy time for you but I would like to know a bit about you. What do you and Mrs Claus have for Christmas dinner? What do you do during the summer? What's your favourite television programme? Have you ever broken the speed limit in your sleigh?

**Lauren, 8**

Dear Santa,

I have some questions for you. What do you wear for the rest of the year? How old were you when you realised you were different from the other children? Is being Santa like being Superman? Are you really nice and jolly or do you have a really bad temper?

Love, Deena

Please answer Santa,

1st. How many hours does it take to deliver the presents to each house

2nd. What are the names of each reindeer, I know ones Red Nose.

Christopher

# Santa – Personal

Dear Santa,

I like Father Christmas. He brings presents and he is a secret man and when happy people get up in the morning they rap up all the papers and they see their presents and its snowing.

Harjinder, 5

Dear Santa,

How are you about Christmas Eve. Well I have been good for Christmas and I would like a Playstation and Ho! Ho! Ho! to you Santa.

Merry Christmas, Edward

I have not forgot to leave my dummy out for the baby reindeers like I said I would when you were visiting Meadowhall Shopping Centre, and I have not had it since I saw you 2 weeks ago.

**Love, Oliver**

Dear Santa,

I am 10 years old by the way. Oh yes you probably know that because you're Santa.

**Kate**

Dear Santa,

I just want to tell you a bit of me. I have got brades and I am brown and I am a girl and you are a boy.

Happy Christmas, Michelle

Dear Santa,

   Thank you for all the presents you will leave me on Christmas Eve and I promise I will sleep all night and not get up too early. We will leave you some goodies although I think sherry is out of the question as Daddy said it is naughty to drink and drive.

Love, Elizabeth

Dear Father Christmas,

   I despaly want a little Andrex puppy. I love them they are ever so cute. I will love him for ever not just for Christmas. There will be a bottle of milk and 10 carrots and 2 mice pies waiting for you and the raindeers so please get me one of the presents I want espelly the puppy. Love from your best customer.

                    Sarah

Dear santa,

How are you? Are your reindeers fit to deliver my presents? I want a Playstation and a real set of money please.

Merry Christmas, Michael

Dear Santa,

I bet your elves get tired nearly every day. I bet you are round and fat from eating all the mince pies and drinking milk. Tell Rudolph to save his nose for Christmas day. Are you magic? I think you could do with a lot of sleep.

Love, Natalie

Dear Santa,

I would like a snooker table and a new football, also a lot more but my mum hasn't got time to look through the Argos. I am saying goodbye now because my mum wants to post this letter.

Thank you, Charlie

Dear Father Christmas,

I hope you are well and I hope your elves are well as well. Would you mind if you thanked them for making the toys for the children. I do hope you dont catch a cold otherwise you will have to get someone to take over, and if that happened we might not get anything, it could all go wrong.

Lots of kisses and cuddles, Hannah

Dear Santa Clause,

   How are you and what have you been doing this year? Busy I'd say but that's for you to say. Is Rudolph's nose still red or has he gone to the desert? Well less about the reindeers how is the misses? Yes I have been good this year. OK maybe a little trouble.

   **Best wishes, Nicky**

Dear Santa,
   How are you? I like your reindeer. Did you lose some weight?

   **Love from Joe**

Dear Father Christmas,

How are you doing? I've had a cold and I passed it on to my little brother! Does Rudolph still have a shiney red nose? I did when I had a cold. Do you shave? I don't bother because I'm only 10 years old.

Yours, Jamie, 10

Dear Santa,

How are you this year? Is Rudolph and the Reindeer? It must be really anoying getting up very early and having to go round the world and be back before morning.

Claire, 10

# Families

Dear Santa,
    I have no pets only my
mam and dad.

Sarah, 7

Dear Father Christmas,

I wanted to send a carrot to Rudolph but Mummy said that you look after him and my carrot may go off in the post. I have been very good this year, kept my room tidy and helped Mummy and Daddy with the gardening and vegetable plot, not been horrible to my sister (more than she deserves).

Penny, 6³/₄

Dear Santa,

It has been a long year. I have tried not to fight with Rosey but it's natrul.

Imogen

Dear Santa Claus,

   I've tried very hard to be good this year but it doesn't come easy with a younger sister Kitty. She's only 4 but she's a monster. She acts like she's 16 using my make-up and clothes. I sometimes feel like strangling her. But let's cut the chit chat and get to the presents . . .

**All my love, Lauren**


My mum done the writing as I can't write good yet.

**Luke**

Dear Father Christmas,

My name is Emma and my sister's name is Josie. She is only 9 months old so she wasn't here last Christmas.

Dear Santa,

My name is Matthew. This Christmas from you I want a car, some sweets and lots of surprises. I saw you last week with my mum.

Dear Father Christmas,

We hope you have had a good long rest since last year. Our daddy would like a tie and our mummy would love a tidy-up machine.

**Wrap up warm, Harry**

Dear Santa,

Please give my mum and dad a brain.

**From Akira**

Dear St Nickolas,

 I am writing to tell you how much me and my family enjoy Christmas. We'll start off telling you how much my mum loves Christmas. She gets very excited. She is always saying 'are you excited?' Next I'll tell you about Dad at Christmas. He gets extremely excited and says the same method as my mum, 'are you excited?' My brother is always answering that question with 'yep'. He never sounds as tho he is. And me, well I enjoy Christmas the same as everyone else.

**Love from Louise**

P.S. I haven't written a list because you always bring me nice things.

father christmas

Dear Santa Claus,

I wish my grann's leg would not hurt please. Father Christmas how did you become Father Christmas? I hope you have a lovely Christmas.

Love, Bianca

Dear Santa,

This year I am spending Christmas over at my Grandmar and Grandpars house, they live in a bungalow down in Devon, you know the one with the garden knonbs. I'm not looking forward to visiting them because there house smells rather horrid.

# And Finally

Dear Santa,

Advent is a time when we get redy for Christmas. Not only do we put decoration up but we get redy in our soals.

Callum

Dear Father Christmas,

Please could you come round to my house on Christmas Eve. My name is Lee and I am a boy and I will be nine on 15 December. If you want to leave me a small present that is alright by me.

Merry Christmas Ho Ho Ho, Lee

Dear Santa,

Please can I have an Animal Hospital Adopshan Center and some books please. And a train set for my dad.

Love, Holly, 8 today

Dear Santa,

I hope youre feeling well. Can you get Barbie for Christmas because my mum hasn't got much money. If you can get that I can be happy. How is Rudolph is he bothering you. I hope he is not.

Love, Aisha, 8

P.S. Why do they call Santa Saint Nickerless?
Answer, because he don't wear no nickers.

Elizabeth, 8

Dear Santa,

Please may I have an orange yoyo which can change colour when you do sleeps and orange roller blades and I really really want an orange mountain bike.

Thanks and I really mean it, Samantha

Dear Santa,

I would like to deliver presents with you and I would like to sit on your reindeers. I would like to see you every night and day.

Lots of love, Kathleen

Dear Father Christmas,

Please I wish I could cuddle you.

Love, Keith

Dear Father
Christmas,
    Would it
please be
possible for
me to have
a Winnie
the Pooh book
for Christmas. I'm
54 years old but I would
really love one.

Love, Paula

Dear Santa

Thank you for all the years you have visited me. As a 16½ year old I think Mum and Dad can take over now.

Thanks. Bye bye, Rachel